SEQUENCING STORIES

Building with Blocks

MEG GAERTNER

The Child's World®
childsworld.com

Published by The Child's World®
1980 Lookout Drive • Mankato, MN 56003-1705
800-599-READ • www.childsworld.com

Photographs ©: Shutterstock Images,
cover (left), cover (middle left), cover
(middle right), cover (right), 3 (left), 3
(right), 5, 6, 9, 10, 13, 14, 17, 18, 21

ISBN 9781503835122
LCCN 2018962891

Printed in the United States of America
PA02425

j
720
G119b

About the Author

Meg Gaertner is a children's
book author and editor who
lives in Minnesota. When not
writing, she enjoys dancing and
spending time outdoors.

CONTENTS

Building Time!

Eric's dad is an **architect**. He **designs** buildings and bridges. Eric has always wanted to be an architect. He decides he will start practicing now. He will build something out of blocks.

Building with blocks is good practice for becoming an architect.

5

Having an idea
is the first step in
building something.

First, Eric thinks about what he wants to build. A house isn't big enough. A bridge isn't cool enough. All at once, he has an idea. He will build a huge **skyscraper**!

Before he begins building, Eric gathers all of his blocks. They come in many different colors and shapes. They will be perfect for his skyscraper.

You can build with
many different
types of blocks.

The shape of a tower can help make it strong.

Right away, Eric starts building the **base**. He wants his skyscraper to be sturdy and tall. He makes a wide base to support the tower.

Next, Eric builds the middle and top sections of the tower. He uses blocks of many different colors. He wants each block to be just right.

Fun Fact

Most blocks are squares or rectangles. But triangles can hold the most weight.

You can build and
rebuild until it is just right.

13

What else could Eric
add to his tower?

Then, Eric adds the final details to his tower. He places the last few blocks on top. He sits back and looks at his tower. Something seems to be missing.

Suddenly, Eric knows what he needs.

He decides his skyscraper needs a fence.

The fence will be the finishing touch.

He builds the fence out of blocks.

Architects plan the fence
and grounds around
their buildings, too.

17

18

How tall can you
build a tower?

At last, the skyscraper is complete. It is tall. It is colorful. It is an amazing building!

Fun Fact

In 2019, the tallest building in the world was the Burj Khalifa. It is in the United Arab Emirates. It is more than 160 floors high.

Eric had a great time building! He will keep building with blocks. He will keep working hard. One day, he will finally be an architect like his dad.

What should Eric build next?

21

Glossary

architect (AR-ki-tekt) An architect is someone who designs buildings. Eric wants to be an architect like his dad.

base (BAYSS) The base is the lowest part of something. Eric built a wide base for his skyscraper.

collapse (kuh-LAPS) To collapse is to fall down suddenly. A building that isn't strong enough could collapse.

designs (di-ZINES) Someone who designs something draws the plans for making it. An architect designs buildings.

skyscraper (SKYE-skray-pur) A skyscraper is a very tall building. Eric decided to build a skyscraper out of blocks.

To Learn More

BOOKS

Mooney, Carla. *Building with Shapes*. Vero Beach, FL: Rourke Educational Media, 2013.

Schwartz, Ella. *Make This!* Washington, DC: National Geographic Society, 2019.

Thomsen, Amanda. *The Big Book of Backyard Adventures: Get Messy, Get Wet, Build Cool Things, and Have Tons of Wild Fun! 51 Free-Play Activities*. North Adams, MA: Storey Publishing, 2019.

WEBSITES

Visit our website for links about building with blocks:
childsworld.com/links

Note to Parents, Teachers, and Librarians: We routinely verify our Web links to make sure they are safe and active sites. So encourage your readers to check them out!

Index